GIANTS MONSTERS & Mythical BEASTS

CONTENTS

D1275579

A READ-ABOUT

Introduction

Since time began, people all over the world have told stories about weird and fantastic creatures. Originally, these stories may have been based on strange sightings or happenings, or they may have been told to try to explain things that were difficult to understand, like thunder.

Over the years, the stories have been shaped by different storytellers until the characters have become legendary.

GIANTS

Most cultures have stories about giants. Usually, they are frightening characters who terrorize people. However, some of these stories end showing the giant to be a simple fellow easily tricked, or a gentle creature willing to make friends.

Because most giants appear in stories and legends, they are commonly thought to be make-believe. But in the 1870s, a fossilized giant was discovered in Ireland. He was 3.70 m (10 ft) tall, and would have weighed about 275 kilos (600 lbs).

Some Well-Known Giants

Cyclops was a famous Greek giant. According to the story, Cyclops was supposed to be particularly terrifying because he had only one eye, set in the middle of his forehead.

The Greeks also told stories about *Atlas*, who was so big and strong that he was able to carry the whole sky on his back. Our word *atlas* comes from his name.

Many great landforms have been attributed to giants. The legend of *Paul Bunyan* began as a collection of yarns told by American lumberjacks in the 1800s. Unlike many giants, Paul Bunyan was a friendly and heroic character. With his friends Babe the Blue Ox and Johnny Inkslinger, he is said to have shaped many land features, including the Grand Canyon.

Giants are said to have played with stones. It was giants, some say, who built the famous stone circle at Stonehenge, in southern England.

"Giant" landmarks like the White Horse in Berkshire can still be seen in England today.

Some giants have places named after them. An English giant named *Bel* declared he would ride from Mountsorrel to Leicester in three leaps. But at his third leap, the journey proved too much for him, and he and his horse dropped dead. The site of Bel's unfortunate end is now the town of *Belgrave* (or Bel's grave).

Mountsorrel

Wanlip

Birstall

Belgrave

5

The mountain people of the Himalayas tell stories of huge creatures known as *abominable snowmen*, or *yetis*. They are said to be about 2 m (7 ft) tall and covered with hair.

There have been many expeditions to find a yeti, but none has been successful, though huge footprints have been found in the snow. Some scientists believe the yetis may, in fact, be the last survivors of a giant gorilla-like ape called *Gigantopithecus*.

People in remote parts of Russia and China have also reported seeing similar wild, hairy creatures. In Russia, they are called *Almas*; while in China, they are known as *Hsing-Hsing*. In North America, there have been many stories about a huge, hairy, human-like creature called *Bigfoot* or *Sasquatch*.

MONSTERS

*L*ike giants, monsters frequently appear in myths, legends, and stories. Many monsters seem to have lived in water. Ancient sailors and explorers often returned home with frightening stories of gigantic sea monsters and sea serpents.

It is known that large creatures such as *plesiosaurus* and *kronosaurus* existed on earth many thousands of years ago. Perhaps it was the discovery of the bones of these that originally gave rise to the stories of so many so-called monsters.

The Loch Ness Monster

Most countries of the world have stories about monster-like creatures.

For hundreds of years, people have claimed to have seen a strange monster swimming in a cold, deep lake in Scotland called Loch Ness.

Scientists have used underwater cameras and sonar equipment to search the lake, but no one has proved whether *Nessie*, the Loch Ness Monster, really exists. Perhaps, in the misty murkiness of Loch Ness, an otter swimming in the lake could be taken for the head of the monster.

The Taniwha

The Maori people of Aotearoa (New Zealand) tell interesting stories about the *taniwha*. It is often described as a fierce, dragon-like creature that lived in deep water and dark places.

The Bunyip

The Australian Aborigines tell stories about a great monster that lived in swamps and pools. They called it the *bunyip*. It was covered with either feathers or fur, and had a roaring voice. Instead of legs, it had flippers with which it made great splashes if it became angry.

Amazing Mythical

Myths and legends from all over the world tell of many strange and fabulous beasts. You would be very unlikely to come across any such creatures today, but many of these stories may be based on animals people really did see.

For centuries, people have told stories about dragons.

Dragons

The dragons of Europe were supposed to have long scaly bodies, sharp claws, huge wings, a snake-like head, and a mouth that could shoot flames.

People believed they really did exist, too. Unexplored places on old maps read *Here Be Dragons*.

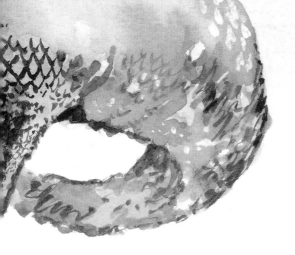

In ancient times, people journeying as far as Africa or India would bring back terrifying stories of strange beasts that could crush you by wrapping themselves around you (pythons) or kill you with their terrible jaws (crocodiles). Perhaps in people's minds these animals were put together to become the single monster they called a *dragon*.

The Unicorn

The *unicorn* is a beautiful mythical beast, existing only in stories. The horn of a unicorn is supposed to have magical properties. In olden days, alchemists sometimes made expensive potions from what they said was ground unicorn horn. If you were to drink from unicorn horn, people said you would be protected from poison. The kings of France traditionally used cups made from the horns of unicorns right up until the French Revolution in 1789. However, it has since been proved that these cups were, in fact, made from rhinoceros horn!

In Greek and Roman times, stories about the unicorn suggested that it came from somewhere in distant India. Perhaps the storytellers were confusing it with the Indian rhinoceros (left) or the Arabian oryx (far left), animals with horns that may have given rise to the legend.

15

The *phoenix* is another strange mythical creature. According to the ancient legend from Egypt, this eagle-like bird appeared only once every five hundred years. It would fly straight to a temple in Heliopolis, where it would settle on the flaming altar and be burned alive. Yet according to the story, it didn't die; for out of the ashes a new phoenix would appear and fly away for another five hundred years.

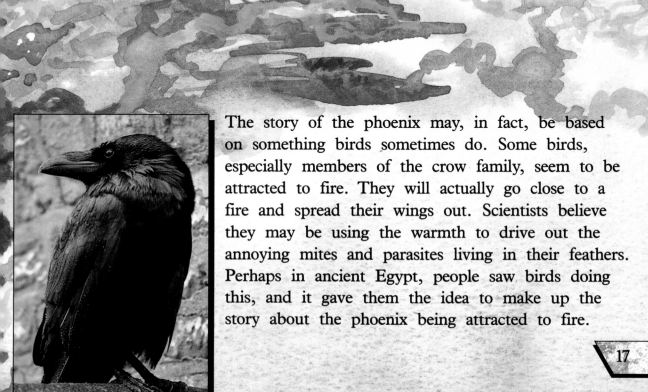

The story of the phoenix may, in fact, be based on something birds sometimes do. Some birds, especially members of the crow family, seem to be attracted to fire. They will actually go close to a fire and spread their wings out. Scientists believe they may be using the warmth to drive out the annoying mites and parasites living in their feathers. Perhaps in ancient Egypt, people saw birds doing this, and it gave them the idea to make up the story about the phoenix being attracted to fire.

The Roc

Sometimes stories about strange monsters and fabulous creatures may, in fact, be partly true.

In the story of "Sinbad the Sailor" from *The Arabian Nights*, we learn how Sinbad finds himself on an uninhabited island in the Indian Ocean. He discovers a *roc*'s egg, an egg so huge that he has to take fifty paces just to walk around it.

The gigantic mother roc or "elephant bird" arrives. She is so big, she blocks out the sun! But our hero, Sinbad, does not worry. He daringly escapes from the island by tying himself to one of the roc's talons with his turban!

ARABIA

AFRICA

INDIAN
OCEAN

MADAGASCAR

N
W E
S

0   800   1600km

500   1000 mi

The story of the roc is too far-fetched to be true. But it may be based on fact. If Sinbad had sailed due south in the Indian Ocean, he would have come to the island of Madagascar, now the Malagasy Republic. Although rocs are now extinct, there were plenty of big birds living over a thousand years ago when the story of "Sinbad the Sailor" was first written.

The Griffin

Some mythical beasts were a combination of two animals. One such creature, the *griffin*, was very strange indeed. It is said to have had the body of a lion, the head and wings of an eagle, and feathers on its back. Its claws were so big people used them as goblets.

Griffins were said to have originated in India. They had a keen eye for gold, which they used to build their nests. They also knew how to find treasure and guarded it fiercely from hunters.

The Centaur

With the head and torso of a man and the body and legs of a horse, the *centaur* belongs to the myths of Ancient Greece. Centaurs were friendly and well-respected by the Greeks.

One centaur, Chiron, was very wise and became a great teacher. He taught archery and music to the sons of kings and many great heroes. When he died, Jupiter, the ruler of the gods, placed him in the sky as the constellation we call *Sagittarius*.

Most of the time, they come from people's imaginations. But even our imagination has to get its ideas from somewhere. These characters often start out as very ordinary everyday creatures, but the storyteller exaggerates to make the story more exciting. We like to be frightened (just a little bit!), as long as we know it's only a story. When the listener tells the story to someone else, it gets even more exaggerated. And so on...

...ut Giants, Monsters,
...ome From?

Maybe that is where these creatures really belong – in the wonderful world of stories.

Index